Learn to Play the UKULELE

Learn to Play the
UKULELE

A SIMPLE AND FUN GUIDE FOR COMPLETE BEGINNERS

BILL PLANT & TRISHA SCOTT

Fox Chapel
PUBLISHING

WHO WE ARE

We are Australians Bill Plant and Trisha Scott. We have taught hundreds of beginners to play the ukulele and have learned a little about teaching along the way. We sing and play a number of instruments, but the ukulele has become our favorite. From our home in Wangaratta, a small town a few hours north of Melbourne, Australia, we travel, play, and teach at music festivals. We like nothing better than playing music with others around a campfire.

Authors Bill Plant and Trisha Scott.

The photos on the following pages have been used under the following Creative Commons licenses: 22 (Nicky Mehta) and 23 (Zooey Deschanel and Jason Mraz) under Attribution 2.0 Generic (CC BY 2.0); 23 (Steven Tyler) under Attribution-ShareAlike 2.0 Generic (CC BY-SA 2.0); 26 under Attribution 3.0 Unported (CC BY 3.0); 31 under Attribution-ShareAlike 3.0 Unported (CC BY-SA 3.0); 57 (Tiny Tim) under Attribution-ShareAlike 2.5 Generic (CC BY-SA 2.5). To learn more, visit *http://creativecommons.org/licenses*.
CD instrumentalists: Bill Plant, Trisha Scott, and Luke R. Davies (12-bar blues)
CD vocalists: Bill Plant, Trisha Scott, and Carmel Carmody (Ukulele Lady)
CD Harmonica: Luke R. Davies
Special thanks to Luke R. Davies and Mike Couch for their assistance with the sound engineering and CD production.
Thanks to Peter Hurney (Pohaku Ukulele), Chuck Moore, and Gary Zimnicki for the use of the photos on page 15.
Special thanks to Jake Shimabukuro and Josh Page of Shore Fire Media for the use of the photograph appearing on page 11.
Thanks to Eric Bogle for the use of the song "Aussie BBQ" on page 54.
Thanks to Deb Neill for the use of the photo on page 60.
Thanks to Ian Fisk for the photos appearing on pages 13, 42, and 59.

ISBN 978-1-56523-687-5

Library of Congress Cataloging-in-Publication Data

Scott, Trisha.
Learn to play the ukulele / Trisha Scott and Bill Plant.
p. cm.
Includes index.
ISBN 978-1-56523-687-5
1. Ukulele--Methods--Self-instruction. I. Plant, Bill. II. Title.
MT645.8.S36 2012
787.8'9193--dc23
2011031480

The authors wrote this song just for you to help you practice. See page 41 for the chord changes, and listen for it on the CD as a bonus track.

IF YOU'RE SICK OF THE TV, YOU GOT NOTHIN' TO DO,
WELL LISTEN UP, BABY, WE'VE GOT SOMETHING FOR YOU,
YOU CAN LEARN THE UKULELE, YOU CAN LEARN IT OVERNIGHT,
SO OPEN UP THE BOOK AND WE'LL SHOW YOU HOW TO DO IT RIGHT,
FIRST YOU TUNE UP YOUR UKE AND THEN YOU LEARN HOW TO STRUM,
YOU DRIVE THE CAT CRAZY WITH THAT BROTHER JOHN,
AND YOUR FINGERS ARE HURTIN', AND YOUR ARM IS GETTIN' NUMB,
THE BOOK HAS THE NERVE TO TELL YOU THAT THIS IS ALL FUN!
IT'S OK FOR THE AUTHORS, 'CAUSE THEY KNOW ALL THE CHORDS,
BUT WE GOTTA PRACTICE 'TIL WE'RE TOTALLY BORED,
THEN THERE'S A SCALE PENTATONIC, WHATEVER THAT MAY BE,
THERE'S EVEN 4/4 TIME AND SOMETHING CALLED THE KEY OF C.
BUT THE SONGS AIN'T HALF BAD IF YOU CAN JUST STRUM ALONG,
THERE'S THE MIDNIGHT SPECIAL AND A SLOOP CALLED JOHN,
I KNOW I'LL LEARN TO PLAY, IT WON'T TAKE ME LONG.
I'LL LEARN TO LOSE THESE, LEARN TO PLAY THE UKULELE…

…OVERNIGHT BLUES.

Contents

ON PAPER: THE BOOK

IN YOUR EAR: THE CD

TRACKS FOR PRACTICE

SONGS TO PLAY

Introduction

When you learn to play the ukulele, you begin your journey as a musician, grasp the nuances of the craft, and find the joy of communicating with other people. This journey is one of the great joys of music. We cannot describe the feeling music will bring to you, but we can help you reach it by showing you how to play the ukulele. Keep playing and you will find the joy for yourself.

We will show you how to play, even if you have no musical experience whatsoever. And if you can play, you will find many tips to improve your technique and help you become a better musician.

Ukulele Fact:

The ukulele became popular because of its portability and versatility. It's also easy to play and above all, fun.

Always remember that you are here to learn to play music, and the learning experience should be stress-free. Relax. Aim to play music with your very first song. Not only will that set a pattern for your practice, it will allow you to enjoy watching your musical ability improve with each practice session. Don't rush to master the book, but progress at your own pace and make beautiful music along the way. When you are relaxed and enjoying the music, your progress will be swift indeed.

In each of the following chapters, we present a different playing technique, so that with regular practice you can easily graduate from beginner to accomplished musician. To help you, we've included a CD with songs chosen for their range of style, strumming patterns, playing techniques, and rhythm. First, you will learn an easy one-finger chord song. Then, you will progress through the chord families and on to bar chords. The sections on rhythm and strumming begin with a simple strumming pattern and easy rhythm, and progressively become more complex. This will encourage you to develop a flexible approach to strumming, which will give your music interesting tonal variations. The chapter on finger picking takes you beyond playing melodies by rote and teaches you how to use the fret board to improvise a melody. There are even sections on the 12-bar blues and a comprehensive chord chart.

Progress is easy, and taking things at your own pace allows you to put your personal stamp on a song and develop your own unique musical style. The tips on practice can be adapted to fit your own needs as you grow as a musician. When you revisit a chapter, you will quickly see how far you have come in just a few practice sessions.. Soon you will be ready to play with other musicians and can look forward to a lifetime of musical enjoyment.

Learning to play music is a life-long journey that never ends. Go slowly, listen to the music you make, and enjoy it from the start. Along the way you will face challenges, experience breakthroughs, occasionally become frustrated, and have moments of pure joy.

It is a journey that will change your life.

—BILL PLANT AND TRISHA SCOTT

Play time. You are never too young or too old to make music a part of your life. Whether you're just learning to talk or on the verge of retirement, playing an instrument like the ukulele can bring you a special kind of joy.

The Hall of Fame

Since its founding in 1996, the Ukulele Hall of Fame Museum has inducted the following individuals: David Kalakaua, Ernest Kaai, Manuel Nunes, Roy Smeck, May Singhi Breen, Cliff Edwards, Sam Kamaka, Arthur Godfrey, Eddie Kamae, Jesse Kalima, Jonah Kumalae, Augusto Dias, Johnny Marvin, Jose do Espirito Santo, Bill Tapia, George Formby, Frank Henry Martin, Herb Ohta, and Lyle Ritz.

CHAPTER 1

Some Basic Ukulele Background

Before you rush out to a music store to purchase a ukulele, or dive into your very first practice session, here's some history and practical information that you might want to consider. It's always good to understand the instrument you are about to play; it will help you know its good qualities and difficulties and allow you to play your best.

Ukulele Fact:

The ukulele is the Hawaiian version of a traditional Portuguese instrument.

A BRIEF HISTORY

The first ukuleles were built in Hawaii in the 1870s by Portuguese immigrants who arrived to work in the sugarcane fields. A small guitar-like instrument from their home country inspired their design for the ukulele. The name ukulele roughly translates as "jumping flea," which describes the fast movement of the musician's fingers over the strings. Hawaiians loved the sound of the ukulele; even Hawaiian royalty took to playing it. Its popularity spread throughout the islands, then worldwide.

In 1915, the ukulele was shown at the Panama Pacific International Exhibition, a world's fair in San Francisco attended by millions of people from around the globe. The ukulele was such a hit that it quickly spread throughout the United States and then across the Atlantic to the United Kingdom.

The ukulele quickly became one of the most popular instruments of the Jazz era. Millions of ukuleles were produced, snapped up by amateur parlor musicians. Performers like George Formby, Arthur Godfrey, and Roy Smeck helped popularize ukulele music. If you want some inspiration, watch these players on YouTube. (You can also catch some modern masters, such as the Ukulele

Orchestra of Great Britain and Jake Shimabukuro, shown below; his version of "While My Guitar Gently Weeps" has had more than three million hits.)

Interest in the ukulele began to decline in the 1950s as rock and roll became dominant and the guitar surged in popularity. But in the 1990s the ukulele made a comeback, featured in stage acts by artists such as Van Morrison and Eddie Vedder and by bands such as Portishead and Florence and the Machine.

Frank Skinner and Lee Evans both close their acts with a ukulele song. The ukulele even made it to the nationally popular TV show *American Idol*, where Jason Castro became the first contestant to play the instrument while singing; he performed "Over the Rainbow."

Ukulele clubs have sprung up all over the world. A quick Internet search on *http://ukulelehunt.com* produces information on twenty-five festivals. Song lyrics and chords are also available for download, usually for free. Check out page 62 for some other great ukulele websites you can visit.

Jake Shimabukuro

Jake Shimabukuro is often credited with sparking the current ukulele craze. A true ukulele virtuoso, Shimabukuro first started playing the instrument when he was four years old, learning with traditional Hawaiian music. He quickly discovered his love for the pop hits and rock songs he heard on the radio and started to teach himself to play his favorites on the ukulele. This fusion of musical traditions has become a striking feature of Shimabukuro's playing, as he continues to seamlessly blend musical styles from classical to rock. The Hawaiian native gained popularity in Honolulu and the island of Oahu, but his performance of "While My Guitar Gently Weeps," recorded in Central Park for a New York TV show, skyrocketed his career after it hit YouTube. The video's popularity brought the ukulele to the attention of millions, along with Shimabukuro's fresh new style. Shimabukuro has appeared on "The Late Show with Conan O'Brien," "The Today Show," "Last Call with Carson Daily," and in Adam Sandler's movie *Just Go With It*. He has also performed with music legends Jimmy Buffett, Bela

PHOTO BY SENCAME.

Ukulele virtuoso Jake Shimabukuro, pictured here playing a Kamake Ukulele Tenor, is known throughout the world for his upbeat and fresh musical style.

Fleck, Bette Midler, Yo-Yo Ma, Cyndi Layper, and Ziggy Marley. To learn more, visit *jakeshimabukuro.com* and *shorefire.com/clients/jshimabukuro*.

PARTS OF THE UKULELE

A) **Head:** The top end of the neck, where the tuners are located.

B) **Tuners:** Straight pegs or geared tuners used to tighten or loosen the strings.

C) **Strings:** Numbered 1 to 4, with number 1 being on the bottom or the right side. Strings are typically tuned to the notes A, E, C, and G.

D) **Nut:** A strip of bone, plastic, or wood that has slots to hold the strings in position.

E) **Frets:** Raised metal strips along the fingerboard, which effectively shorten a string when it is pressed down over a fret.

F) **Neck:** Includes the fingerboard, which has reference dots to indicate the fret positions.

G) **Body:** The hollow box that magnifies the sound of the vibrating strings, creating the instrument's tone.

H) **Sound hole:** Where the sound exits.

I) **Bridge:** The anchor point for the strings.

TYPES OF UKULELES

Ukuleles come in different shapes and sizes, producing all kinds of sounds and tones. If you want an upbeat bright sound, you'll want to use a soprano ukulele, but for something more mellow, consider a concert ukulele.

Soprano. This is the smallest ukulele and also the most popular size. Its light, bright tone is well suited to vocals.

Concert. This ukulele's tone is deeper and more mellow than the soprano, and it has a slightly longer neck with wider fret spacing. Those with large fingers will find it easier to play than the smaller soprano. It also sounds good with vocals.

Tenor. The second-largest ukulele, the tenor is loud and needs to be played softly as an accompaniment.

Baritone. The largest type of ukulele, the baritone has a deep sound that makes it a wonderful addition to a group of ukuleles.

BUYING ADVICE

There is a wide range of ukuleles on the market, made from solid wood, laminated wood, fiberboard, plastic, or a combination of these materials. Price can range from a few dollars to many thousands, but cost does not always indicate quality and tone.

If you are buying your first ukulele, take an experienced player along to help you choose. Look for a music store with a range of ukuleles tuned and ready to play. If you go to a store where the ukuleles are still in boxes or un-tuned, the staff might not be as knowledgeable about the instrument and will not be able to guide you in your selection.

Take your time and listen to as many instruments as possible. You will find a marked variation in the quality of sound between ukuleles, even between those of the same brand and model. A solid wood instrument will actually improve and become more mellow with age and use. Keep this in mind when you are considering your options. Most inexpensive ukuleles come with poor quality strings and will benefit from a set of synthetic nylon strings like Aquila Nylgut or Worth. (When you replace the strings, change one at a time so you can copy the original knot sequence.)

Purchase the best instrument you can afford with the best tone and best action. (Action refers to the distance between the strings and the frets; a well-constructed instrument is easy on the fingers and a delight to play.) A local music store is probably the best place to begin. Avoid online sales of second-hand ukuleles unless you can try the instrument first, and keep in mind that a serious musician rarely sells a good instrument.

Custom Ukuleles

When you begin playing, it is probably best to buy a ukulele from a local music shop. Then, when you find that you really enjoy playing (and we know you will), consider investing in a higher-quality instrument, possibly even one that is custom-made. There are instrument-makers all over the world who are dedicated to producing beautiful, one-of-a-kind ukuleles that are beautiful to look at and beautiful to hear. For starters, take a look at the ones on the next page. See page 62 for a list of some of our favorite makers.

Ukulele Tip:

Visit ukulele forums before buying; see what others are saying about the brand you're considering.

Bold White, 2007. Concert ukulele made of koa, maple, and rosewood. Created by Peter Hurney, Pohaku Ukulele.

Concert ukulele with a 7⅞" (200mm) lower body width and a 15¼" (387mm) scale length. Koa body, ebony fretboard, peghead veneer, rosewood bridge, and friction peg tuners. Created by Gary Zimnicki.

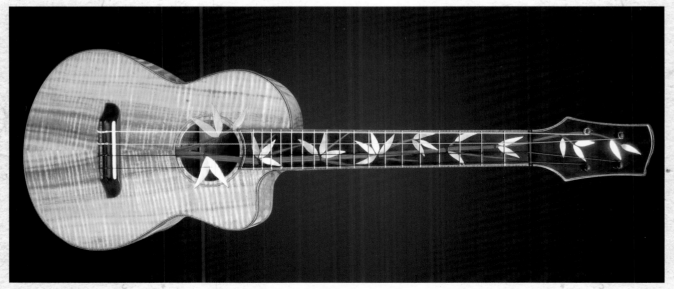

Cutaway tenor ukulele. Blonde koa with bamboo, gold mother of pearl, and bloodwood inlay. Created by Chuck Moore.

CHAPTER 2

How to Hold and Tune a Ukulele

Before you get down to playing, there are some things you need to know about using your ukulele. First, you'll need to learn how to hold it comfortably, so that it's easy for you to play. Then you'll need to learn how to tune the strings, so no matter what you're practicing, it will sound great.

Be gentle. Use your right arm to cradle the body of the ukulele and your left hand to grasp the neck lightly.

HOLDING YOUR UKULELE

Hold the body of the ukulele against you with your right forearm, using your left hand to support the neck. Place your hand near the head, with your thumb behind the neck and your fingers curled loosely over the fingerboard, as if you have a small ball in your hand.

Most beginners grip the neck too tightly and push too hard on the strings. The result is stiff fingers and sore fingertips. As you practice, you will become more comfortable with holding and changing the chord shapes. Soon, you will be able to relax your hand and move more freely around the fingerboard. Then, you can try different positions and experiment with the angle at which you hold the neck.

To get the best sound from a ukulele, strum the strings where the neck meets the body, not over the sound hole.

Some players use a strap around their neck to support the ukulele. Avoid this temptation. Try to get by without a strap, and you will soon be comfortable holding your ukulele on your own. All this may seem a bit difficult at first, but with some practice, it will soon become natural for you.

WAYS TO TUNE A UKULELE

A new ukulele is hard to keep in tune, because the strings continually slacken until the knots and windings take up. You must tune and retune the ukulele until it stays in tune right through a practice session. Get in the habit of retuning before each session, listening to each string as you do so. Be aware that any variation in temperature will cause the strings to change length and go out of tune. Be precise with your tuning, because this will help you develop an ear for the ukulele. Pretty soon, you will be able to tune by ear.

There are five different ways to tune a ukulele. All of them work, but for beginners, some are easier than others.

Electronic tuning

The easiest way for a beginner to tune a ukulele is to use an electronic clip-on tuner that "reads" the vibration directly from the instrument and shows the tuning on a display.

The tuner is clipped to the head of the ukulele so it is not influenced by outside sounds, making it ideal for use in a noisy environment. You can purchase an electronic

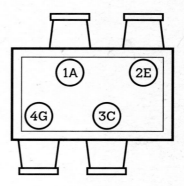

Pitch pipe basics. Pitch pipe showing string number and note.

tuner designed specifically to tune a ukulele, or you can use an electronic chromatic tuner, which can be used to tune any instrument. Electronic tuners have a default frequency of 440 hertz (Hz), so that all instruments tuned using one will be tuned to the same pitch. The frequency on some tuners can be changed inadvertently, so make sure yours is always set to 440Hz. Electronic tuners range in price, but you can expect to pay about $20 for one at your local music store.

Pitch pipe

These inexpensive tuners (generally $10 or less) have four pipes that are numbered and tuned to the pitch of each string on your instrument.

To use the pitch pipe to tune your ukulele, blow into the pipe that corresponds with the string you want to tune. For example, if you are tuning the G string, blow into pipe number four and hum the resulting note out loud. Alternate between humming the note and plucking the string and listen for the difference. If the string sounds too low, tighten it; if it sounds too high, loosen it.

Some Internet sites and phone apps offer an electronic alternative to the standard pitch pipe, generating tuning tones through your computer or phone's speakers.

Tuner basics. A clip-on tuner registers an instrument's pitch based on the vibration of the sound waves rather than the sound itself. It's perfect for tuning up in a noisy place.

Keyboard

You can also tune by ear from a keyboard, starting at middle C. Use the same technique that you would to tune with a pitch pipe: play the note, hum it, then tune the string. Use Track 1: Tuning Reference on the accompanying CD to get some practice using this method.

Listen and Play Along
TRACK 1: TUNING REFERENCE

On this track, you will hear four notes played on the keyboard in the order A, E, C, G. As each note is played, play the corresponding string on your ukulele and tune accordingly, tightening and loosening the string as needed to match the sound of the keyboard notes.

♪ *Tune the A string of your ukulele to the first note played on the keyboard*

♪ *Tune the E string to the second note*

♪ *Tune the C string to the third note*

♪ *Tune the G string to the fourth note*

Another ukulele

You can tune ukuleles to each other in the same manner that you tune to a pitch pipe or keyboard. Have someone play a note on one string of the first ukulele. Hum the note and adjust your ukulele string until the notes match. Continue to copy the tuning, string by string. Remember: play the string, hum the note, and adjust the string.

Tuning fork

You can tune the A-string of your ukulele to a tuning fork, which costs about $20, and then tune the other strings accordingly. Use the diagram at the right as a guide for tuning each string in relation to the others.

Tuning from a keyboard

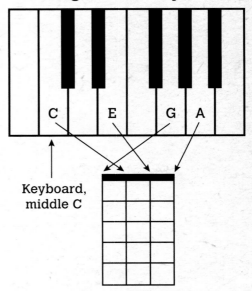

Keyboard, middle C

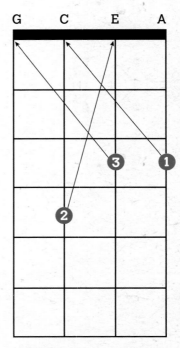

Tune with a tuning fork. First tune the A string to the pitch of the tuning fork. Next, hold down the A string at the third fret and tune the C string, adjusting it until its sound matches the fretted A string. Note the C string is an octave lower than the fretted A string and therefore sounds deeper, but it will match. Next, hold down the C string at the fourth fret and tune the E string. Finally, hold the E string down at the third fret and tune the G string to it.

LET'S PLAY A SONG

Listen and Play Along
TRACK 2: FRÈRE JACQUES

Your starting song is the children's tune "Frère Jacques." This song uses just two fingers: the third finger of your left hand to hold a C major chord shape, and your right index finger to strum a simple downstroke in time to the music. If you think this sounds good, wait until you complete the section on strumming techniques. Then you will sound sensational!

♪ *Start Track 2 on the CD and play along. Tap your foot to keep time, and do your best. Here are the lyrics so you can sing along when you're comfortable:*

Frère Jacques, Frère Jacques,
*   Dormez vous? Dormez vous?*
Sonnez les matines; sonnez les matines,
*   Din din don, Din din don.*
Are you sleeping, are you sleeping?
*   Brother John, Brother John*
Morning bells are ringing, morning bells are ringing,
*   Ding ding dong, ding ding dong.*

C major

The next chapter will cover some more ukulele-playing fundamentals, but if you need a break, skip to the back of the book and try playing a few of the two-chord songs using C major and F major.

C major

F major

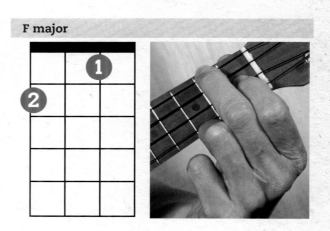

CHAPTER 3

Practice, Practice

I once asked a really good ukulele player how much she practiced. She replied, "When I decided to become a good player, I practiced for five hours a day, but not every day." You may not have five hours to spare, but you will find that just fifteen minutes of practice a day will make a remarkable difference to your playing.

Ukulele Tip:

Remember, the world's finest ukulele players once struggled to play basic chords and melodies.

A FEW BASICS

Set up regular short practice sessions once a day or every other day. New students who try to tackle one or two marathon sessions each week often become discouraged and give up, so take it easy. Play *with* the instrument and focus on making music right from the start. You will be encouraged by the rewards, which will make learning fun and progress steady.

Listen to a song on the CD and read the associated teaching comments. As you listen, clap to find the basic rhythm. When you have the rhythm down, hold the ukulele neck loosely with your left hand to mute the stings and pick up the rhythm as a strumming pattern with your right hand—this is percussion strumming.

Always keep to the beat of the song by tapping your foot. Get out of your chair when you practice. Stand up, stay loose, and move your body to the music. Practicing this way will help you keep the beat and develop a natural tendency to find the rhythm in each song. Your strumming will soon become natural and effortless.

Whenever you play a song, play along with the melody, either from the CD or by singing. Otherwise, you will develop poor timing and your playing will become stilted.

Put down the music book and listen for the chord changes. There is no quicker way to learn than to train your ear. In time, you will be able to play the chords simply by singing or "thinking" the melody. Don't get discouraged if you have trouble at first. You have plenty of time to learn the more complex techniques. Enjoy where you are right now. The rest will soon fall into place.

Once you get the feel of a song and can incorporate your own style into the music, you will really start to develop as a ukulele player. As you work through the book step by step, you will become more proficient by increasing your range of chords and strumming skills. Then, bingo! One day you will have found the secret of music and become a fine ukulele player.

STRUMMING PRACTICE

Make time for percussion strumming practice, playing along with songs on the radio or your iPod. Mute the strings so you don't actually play chords. Tap your foot to the beat and practice a simple strum. Keep at it until you can strum along through an entire song. Once you've mastered this, you can experiment with different strum patterns that match the rhythm and feel of the song. You can even practice this technique on a song before you learn to play it.

By practicing this way, you will quickly develop a wide range of strum patterns and a more relaxed style of playing, which will allow you to respond to changes in rhythm and feel within a song. When you realize you can tackle any rhythm, you will play more confidently.

CHORD PRACTICE

One of the best ways to learn a chord shape is to train your fingers. First, place your fingers on the fingerboard as if you are about to play a chord. Then, lift your fingers ever so slightly so the strings come off the fingerboard. Put your fingers down on the strings again. Repeat this slowly. Then, without looking, lift your fingers a little higher and hold the chord shape again. This trains your finger muscles to memorize the chord shape, something that will eventually become automatic. The next step is to change from one chord to another until you can do that without looking. Then, practice a three-chord progression.

Be bold and try to play difficult chords as soon as you need them for a song. With a little practice, you will find them easier to play than you first thought.

SPEED PRACTICE

It is much better to play at a comfortable speed at which you can change chords, keep time, and enjoy the music rather than race through a song trying to keep up. If you find it difficult to keep up with a song on our CD, listen to it for a while until you learn to sing the melody. Then, play it at your own pace, following the lyrics and chord changes in the book. Your practice sessions will be more enjoyable and your speed will increase naturally.

PHOTO BY NEELIX.

Ukulele stardom. There are lots of singers learning to play the ukulele. *American Idol* season seven contestant Jason Castro, pictured here, performed "Over the Rainbow" while accompanying himself on the ukulele.

PHOTO BY NICK OF CHELMSFORD, ESSEX.

Ukulele popularity. Singer-songwriter Nicky Mehta plays several instruments, including the ukulele, as part of the all-female folk trio the Wailin' Jennys.

SINGING PRACTICE

Just do it. No matter how rusty you are or tuneless you think you sound, sing your heart out every chance you get.

By learning the ukulele, you also learn pitch and melody, which are big parts of playing musical instruments and singing. The rest is about practice. Every time you sing, you strengthen your singing muscles. If you keep at it you will improve remarkably.

Whenever possible, stand up when you sing. This opens your chest cavity and allows you to take deep breaths and use your diaphragm to push the air from your lungs. Your diaphragm, not your throat, lends power to your voice. Standing enables you to move around easily, which will definitely improve your delivery (just watch the backup singers in any band). You do not need to take big gulps of air when you sing. Breathe deeply and gently at each break in the vocals. Imagine that the breath goes all the way down past your belly button.

Relax your throat muscles and sing at a comfortable volume. Don't be tempted to shout, because if you sing too loudly your throat will constrict and choke the sound. You may even do some temporary damage to your throat. To avoid strain, always warm up before a singing session: relax your neck and shoulders, stretch your jaw and face muscles (when no one is watching), practice deep breathing from the diaphragm, and exercise your vocal chords by making a variety of silly sounds up and down the scale (do re mi fa so la ti do, and so on).

Make your singing fun by practicing with songs you enjoy. You'll be amazed at the way you progress and the way your improved singing will also improve your musicality on the ukulele.

PHOTO BY DAIGL OLIVA.

Steven Tyler.

PHOTO BY JOE CEREGHINO.

Zooey Deschanel.

PHOTO BY MOSES NAMKUNG.

Jason Mraz.

Playing with the Stars

Here's a list of ukulele musicians and others who are giving or gave the instrument a try. Now that you're well on your way to becoming a great ukulele player yourself, you can add your name to the list: Bob Hope, Barack Obama, Neil Armstrong, Elvis Costello, Pink, Tony Blair, Bruce Springsteen, Elvis Presley, Holly Hunter, Joni Mitchell, Bette Midler, Shirley Temple, Zac Efron, Eric Clapton, Marilyn Monroe, Steve Martin, Kate Micucci, Lucille Ball, Bill Cosby, Will.i.am (Black Eyed Peas), Jason Mraz, Steven Tyler (Aerosmith), Dave Matthews, Paul McCartney, Eddie Vedder, Warren Buffett, Tom Hanks, Suzi Quattro, Taj Mahal, Pete Townshend, Mia Farrow, Cyndi Lauper, Harry Hill, Jamie Oliver, Robert Plant, George Harrison, Ade Edmondson, Buster Keaton, Adam Sandler, Frank Skinner, Taylor Swift, Tony Danza, and Zooey Deschanel.

CHAPTER 4

Keeping Time and Strumming

One of the keys to playing music well is the ability to find and keep the beat. This might take some time to pick up, as each song has its own individual rhythmic feel and tempo. But, with a little practice, you'll soon be strumming along to the beat of any song and adding your own rhythmic flair.

Ukulele Fact:

A good painting has variation in color, texture, and shading; so should your playing.

BASIC TIME SIGNATURES

A piece of music is divided into measures of time called bars, and each bar contains a certain number of beats. Time signatures appear at the beginning of a piece of music written as two numbers stacked one on top of the other. The top number indicates the number of beats in each bar, while the bottom number indicates which note encompasses a full beat. Music encompasses a great many different time signatures, but for starters, try two of the most basic:

4/4 time

This is the most common time signature, appearing in a piece of music as the figure 4/4 or sometimes as the symbol C, for common time. In 4/4 time, there are four beats per measure, and the quarter note equals one beat.

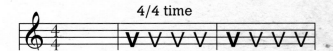

4/4 time

In the illustration above, each *V* in the measures represents a down strum. When strumming in 4/4 time, you can emphasize the first beat of the bar. That is, play it a little louder so the strum goes like this:

ONE/two/three/four, **ONE**/two/three/four,
ONE/two/three/four, and so on.

3/4 time

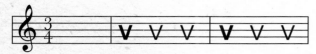

Also known as waltz time, 3/4 time indicates that there are three beats in each measure and the quarter note equals one beat. This time signature is played as follows:

ONE/*two*/*three*, **ONE**/*two*/*three*, **ONE**/*two*/*three*, *and so on.*

Always tap your foot to the beat of the song so that your strumming follows suit. Some songs have rests, or places where there is no strumming at all. Keep tapping your foot to the beat, even through the rests, so when you begin strumming again, you will be able to come in at the correct time and remain on the beat.

STRUMMING

Strumming really lets you shine as a ukulele player. Because there are many techniques and infinite variations, strumming gives you the opportunity to put your own stamp on the music. But beware of *Strum Mania,* a condition that overcomes some players and causes them to play all songs loudly and over the top of the vocals, at the same tempo, and with a "strum machine" rhythm. Everything sounds the same. Don't be tempted to fall into this method of strumming.

F major

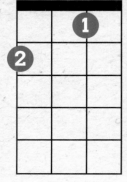

PLAYING CHORDS

Strumming goes hand-in-hand with playing chords—that is, holding down one or more strings to create different notes. When you work on your strumming technique, use the simple C major chord. When you are ready to start practicing chord changes and progressions, use the information in Chapter 5 and the charts on pages 55–57 to learn the chord shapes.

When you play a song, you play a series of different chords to accompany the melody. To make a chord, look at the chord chart, fret the appropriate string or strings, and strum across all the strings. To play a C major chord, hold down the A string at the third fret as the chart to the lower left shows, changing the A string to a C note. This means when you play you will be strumming a C major chord: G, C, E, C. When you reach the song "Polly Wolly Doodle" (page 43, Track 9), you will see a diagram for the two chords used in the song. Letters embedded in the lyrics, which match the names of the chords, tell you when to change from one chord to the other. This switch from one chord to another is called a chord change.

First, learn to play your chord changes on the beat as you play a simple strum to a song. Later, as the chord changes become easy (and they will), you can add variations to the basic strumming pattern. Once the variations become automatic, you can work them into your repertoire. Then, simply by varying the strumming pattern, you will be able to create your own style for each song you play.

If you need some inspiration, watch some really good players on YouTube. Remember that each one of them started out by playing a simple strum, and they undoubtedly struggled with chords.

PRACTICE

Listen and Play Along
TRACK 3: STRUMMING PATTERNS

Exercise 1: *Simple strumming*

Play the following strumming variations in C major in 4/4 time:

♪ *Tap your foot to the beat of the exercise. Strum down to each beat with the nail of your forefinger. Strum as if you are flicking water off your fingernail and you will produce a nice crisp sound. That's it. We told you it was simple.*

♪ *The beat 1/2/3/4 is played by strumming down/down/ down, up/down. The "down, up" means you strum twice on the third beat—once downward, once upward.*

♪ *Now strum twice on the third and fourth beat, making the strumming pattern down/down/down, up/ down, up.*

Exercise 2: *A rest and a choke*

For this exercise, keep time, but do not strum for the first two beats. After the fourth beat, put your fingers over the strings to quickly stop the sound. Here's the strumming pattern:

♪ *rest/rest/up, down/down, choke.*

For a dramatic staccato choke, make a fist and hold it over the strings. Flick your fingers out and down across the strings. As you do that, drop your hand down on the strings.

Exercise 3: *Strumming up high*

Play this strum by brushing your fingers over the fingerboard around the seventh fret:

♪ *down, up/down, up/down, up/down, up.*

Notice that for this strumming pattern, you play two strums on each beat.

Ukulele Tip:

Regular practice with a metronome will improve your timing and ability to play with others.

PHOTO BY FLUTEFLUTE.

Duking it out. Biggar, Scotland, takes pride in its very own ukulele ensemble, known as the Dukes of Uke. Search for similar groups in your area. You might want to attend a performance or see if you can join them for a jam session.

Listen and Play Along
TRACK 4: STRUMMING IN 3/4 TIME

Exercise 1: *Simple strumming in 3/4*

Try the following strumming patterns in 3/4 time, using the C major chord:

♪ *Play this simple strum to the beat 1/2/3: down/down/up, down. On the last beat strum up first, and then down.*

♪ *Vary the strum like this: down/down, up/down.*

Now that you've had some practice strumming in both 4/4 and 3/4 time, come up with a strumming pattern on your own. For example, you might want to try strumming down/down/down, up in 3/4 time. In what other ways can you vary what you've already learned to play?

How to Spell Ukulele

The proper Hawaiian spelling of ukulele is ʻukulele. The open quote mark that appears before the word is called an ʻokina. The ʻokina represents a glottal stop—an interruption of the flow of breath in speech (think of when you say "uh-oh"). The placement of the ʻokina can change the meaning of a word.

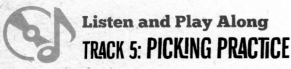

Listen and Play Along
TRACK 5: PICKING PRACTICE

Strumming plays all four strings at once. But there are ways to play, or pluck, one or two strings at a time, which creates a very different kind of sound. Try these exercises to get the hang of several different picking techniques and variations.

Exercise 1: *Simple picking techniques*

♪ *Pluck any two strings by pinching them together and pulling away with your thumb and forefinger.*

♪ *Use your thumb to pluck the G string on the downstroke and any other finger to pluck a different string on the upstroke.*

Exercise 2: *Banjo roll*

You play a banjo roll by plucking three different strings using the thumb, forefinger, and the second finger of your right hand, in that order. Play slowly at first. Try playing several different combinations of strings; some will sound better than others. Don't give the banjo roll too much thought when you play it, just keep playing and listening to your music.

♪ *Start a banjo roll using the technique described previously. Speed up as you get more comfortable.*

Big finish. You often end a song with a tremolo. Hold the ukulele as shown here and strum the same chord repeatedly by moving your second finger over the strings along the neck.

Exercise 3: *Tremolo*

When you play the same note or chord rapidly over and over to sustain its sound, you are playing a tremolo. It sounds great at the end of a song, or when you would like to add a little drama to a certain part of a song. To play a tremolo, hold the ukulele vertically. Place your strum thumb along the neck with your second finger pointing to the bridge. Brush your second finger back and forth across the strings.

♪ *Play a tremolo slowly and cleanly and you will soon speed up.*

♪ *Try playing the tremolo holding the neck at the seventh fret to see how you like the sound.*

♪ *Move your hand up and down the neck to see how the sound changes.*

Exercise 4: *Triplet*

A triplet consists of three strums of equal length that take up one beat: two strums on a downstroke and one strum on an upstroke. Earlier, you played a downstroke and an upstroke on a single beat, but used only your forefinger. To play a triplet, play the downstroke with your forefinger followed by the thumb (in the same strum), and then play the upstroke with your finger. The strokes should be smooth, one right after the other, to make a rhythm of 1-2-3. You might want to repeat the syllables tri-pa-let in your head, playing one note for each syllable, to help you keep the rhythm. Practice playing a triplet the fourth beat of a measure in 4/4 time:

♪ *down/down/down/triplet.*

A triplet is a complex strum, but easy to play slowly, so take it easy at first and gradually build up speed as you practice.

Exercise 5: *Hammer on*

For this exercise, pluck the G string and immediately hammer down with your finger behind the second fret so the note changes while it is still ringing.

Practice until the hammering on comes naturally. Then, try this variation: Hammer on the G string second fret, then strum the resulting A minor chord in 4/4 time. The strumming goes like this:

♪ *Hammer on, up/down, up/down, up/down, up.*

A minor

Exercise 6: *A challenge*

Try this exercise, which combines three different techniques on the last beat—a strum, hammer on, and choke:

♪ *rest/rest/hammer on, up/down, choke.*

Strumming Practice

Make a promise to yourself to practice ten minutes a day for one week playing through each strumming exercise. Play each strum slowly and carefully, and at the end of the week, you will be surprised how well you are doing. Play the exercises for another week, focusing on playing freely with a relaxed strum. Now you are ready to put it all together.

The last section of Track 5 is the song "Pay Me My Money Down" (see page 44), which is played as a percussion exercise. Play along by muting your strings with your fingers so the strum is percussive. If no one is watching, stand up and move your body around in time with the music, sing the vocals, and relax, focusing on getting the feel of the song. Now for that fine performance, just add chords.

Warning: If you find yourself strumming without much thought, never varying the pattern, you have fallen victim to *strum mania*! Rid yourself of this deadly disease by focusing on the song and trying to come up with ways to use your strumming to highlight the vocals.

CHAPTER 5

Scales and Chords

Melodies are often based on a sequential eight-note series called a scale. One of the best examples of a scale comes from *The Sound of Music*, when Julie Andrews sings, "do, re, mi, fa, so, la, ti, do." The name of the scale indicates the note on which it starts. So a C major scale starts on C and continues upward: C, D, E, F, G, A, B, C.

Scales are the lima beans you have to eat before you can have the dessert of playing a melody. For stringed instruments like the ukulele and guitar, scales and melodies are often written in tablature (tabs), which is a way of writing the fret positions of notes on the fingerboard, so you can play them without needing to read music.

SOME COMMON SCALES

Listen and Play Along
TRACK 6: SCALE PRACTICE

On this track, you will hear a C major scale, the song "Twinkle, Twinkle, Little Star," a C major pentatonic scale, and the riff from the song "I've Got Sunshine." Read on to learn about each of these elements. After you read about each one, try to play along with the corresponding section of the track. Remember to keep practicing your scales. Along with chords, these are the building blocks to music.

Ukulele Tip:

A standard guitar pick will limit your strumming; it is best to play without one.

C major scale

With a few exceptions, a song written in the key of C will be made up of notes from the C scale (C, D, E, F, G, A, B, C). The C scale tablature drawing below represents the ukulele fret board. The circles with numbers represent the fret positions, with zero being an open string.

On the diagram of the C major scale, the first symbol means you play the third string open (no fret). The second symbol means you stay on the third string and play the second fret. The next note will be the second string played open, followed by the second string at the first fret, and so on.

The C scale, tablature

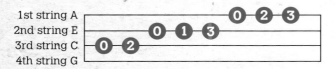

As the diagram indicates, the starting note for this C scale is the open C string, which is the C note, but a C scale can start on a C at any octave.

The C scale fret board drawing below shows another form of tablature for the C scale. In this diagram, the letters in circles indicate the note you will hear when you place your fingers as shown on the fingerboard. So, begin by playing an open C string, then the C string at the second fret, followed by an open E string, and so on.

The C scale fret board

♪ *Listen to the first part of Track 6, a C major scale, and try to play along. Use the two different forms of tablature to help guide you.*

G major scale

The notes in the G major scale are G, A, B, C, D, E, F#, and G. To start the scale, play the second string, holding it on the third fret as the diagram indicates. Next, play the same string, holding it at the fifth fret, and so on.

The G scale, tablature

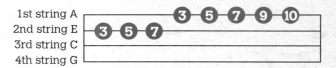

D major scale

Now, try playing a D major scale using the tablature on the diagram below.

The D scale, tablature

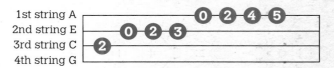

Practice your scales for short periods at a time so you do not become bored and give up on them altogether. Be patient. As you become more fluent with a scale, experiment further up the neck and find scale notes in other fret positions.

Comedy Prop.
The ukulele can be used for all kinds of performances. Comedian and actress Kate Micucci has appeared with the instrument on the hit TV show *Scrubs*, and frequently incorporates it in her comedy act.

PHOTO BY KAFZIEL.

READING TABLATURE AND PLAYING

As you've seen from the previous depictions of the C, G, and D scales, tablature is played from left to right, and the lines in a tablature chart represent the individual strings. Tablature can be typed rather than drawn (see the typed tablature for a C major scale at the right).

♪ *Now that you have an idea of how tablature works, try playing "Twinkle, Twinkle, Little Star" from the tablature at the right. The song is in 4/4 time. An R indicates a rest for a beat.*

Mastering the fingerboard will take time, but if you experiment and listen to your music along the way, you will make good progress; all it takes is time and practice. Be bold and try new techniques. They may be difficult at first, but you will be surprised at how quickly you can learn them.

C major scale

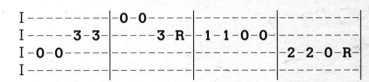

Tinkle, Twinkle, Little Star

PLAYING LEAD BREAKS AND RIFFS

Lead breaks and riffs are just short melodies, usually played with single notes. If you learn them by rote, they can often sound stilted, because your focus tends to be on the riff rather than the timing and feel of the song. If you intend to play a melody by rote, you will need to learn it thoroughly. Better still, learn scales and improvise your own melodies and riffs.

A good example of a riff or run is the note sequence G, A, and B. This sequence can be used to create a transition between a G chord and a C chord. As the tablature at the right shows, you play the notes on the first and second strings.

Bye, Bye, Love

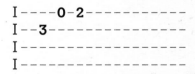

As the diagram above shows, play the second string, third fret, followed by an open first string, then the first string, second fret. Try the sequence again, and follow it with a C major chord. A fine example of this riff can be found on the Everly Brothers recording of "Bye, Bye, Love."

EASY SOLOING WITH A FIVE-NOTE SCALE

The pentatonic (five-note) scale is widely used in all types of music, from rock and roll to classical. It is different from the scales described previously but complements them very well. You can use a pentatonic scale to solo over a chord progression without any clash between the notes of the scale and the chords. For example, you can use a C major pentatonic scale to accompany a C progression of the C, F, and G scales.

To find a pentatonic scale, figure out which notes are numbers 1, 2, 3, 5, 6, and 8 in the 8-note scale. For example, the C pentatonic scale is C, D, E, G, A and C.

♪ *Listen to the third part of Track 6 to hear what a C pentatonic scale sounds like and try to play along. Then, try playing the notes in the tablature below. It happens to be the riff from "I've Got Sunshine" by the Temptations, and is also included as a part of Track 6.*

I've Got Sunshine

```
I-----------0-3----
I-------0-3--------
I---0-2------------
I-----------------
```

A good way to begin playing riffs is to learn the appropriate pentatonic scale fluently, picking with your thumb and forefinger. Follow the tablature and play the first note with a downstroke of your thumb, the second with an upstroke of your forefinger, and so on. Rest your little finger on the front of the ukulele to steady your hand.

Your progress will be slow at first, but keep practicing until you become adept at playing up and down the scale. Take your time. It takes practice to become proficient. When you're feeling pretty confident, play "My Blue Heaven" (page 50, Track 16), a slow song in the key of C. Play notes from the C pentatonic scale at random over the top of the song. You'll find that some of the notes will be right on the melody, while others will be in harmony. Once you get that down, try playing the C pentatonic scale over some other songs in C.

A good way to extend your skills while you watch TV is to try and find notes that match the music from shows and the commercials. There are many key changes in TV audio, and playing along will naturally extend your range. For the sake of domestic harmony, though, make sure no one else is trying to watch the television!

Eventually you will learn fingering patterns on your fret board that are common to all keys. That's just a bonus; all you need to make music is a basic knowledge of chords.

Easy accompaniment. The kazoo is a wonderful instrument to accompany the ukulele, providing a rich brassy sound. Try using one to play the trumpet riff in Johnny Cash's "Ring of Fire."

CHORDS AND CHORD FAMILIES

A chord is a group of three or more notes played together. The word comes from the Middle English "accord." The "key" of a song is named after the chord family or scale used to compose the song, and is designated by a letter: C, G, etc. For example, a song in the key of C is composed primarily of notes from the C scale.

The key determines the pitch of a song, or how high or low it is sung and played. Most songs are played in a key suited to the vocal range of a singer. If you find the pitch of a song too high or too low for your vocal range, you can always change the key.

A basic major chord family in any key consists of three major chords, usually referred to as I, IV, and V. To find the basic chord framework of a key, begin with the key chord (I). Count along the scale to the fourth note, which will form the root of chord IV. Now find the fifth note of the scale, or the root for chord V. These are the main chords you will find in any song.

For the key of C, the chord pattern is C, F, and G or G7 (C is the first note of the scale, F the fourth, and G the fifth).

The V chord will sometimes include a note that is a minor seventh above the root note of the chord, or in other words, the minor seventh note of the root-note scale. For example, the minor seventh of a G chord is F and the minor seventh of a C chord is B flat. Including this note gives the chord a slightly dissonant sad sound. Chords that include the minor seventh note are called dominant seventh chords and are written with a 7 behind the chord name: G7, C7, etc. You might also see them indicated in music as V7. All the seventh chords in this book are dominant sevenths. However, there are many ways to play a seventh chord, including using a major seventh (major seventh chord) or using a minor third and a minor seventh (minor seventh chord). As you progress, try experimenting with these alternative seventh chords and incorporate them into some songs.

The I, IV, and V chords form the basic framework for a great many songs. Some songs include extra chords, called passing chords, added around the melody. There are lots of great three-chord songs that get along fine without passing chords, though.

When Not To Play

As a beginning player, thrilled with your progress, flush with new chords, and all fired up with the beat, you might often sound like hail beating down on a tin roof. You will find that you usually play enthusiastically and loudly, which can mean that you are playing over others in a group or with no feeling for the song.

You will quickly learn, however, that you will perform some of your best music when you listen and play sparingly. Remember this when you are playing. Stop for a moment and listen. Keep your foot tapping to the beat and try to add a note or two or quietly strum a chord.

When backing a singer, do not play over the top of the vocals. Instead, fill a few gaps in between the vocal lines. Do not overdo it. Your time for stardom will come when the rest of the players step back to give you your "break" and allow you to show your stuff.

For the key of C, the chord pattern is C, F, and G or G7:

Notes in the scale	C	D	E	F	G (G7)	A	B	C
Chord number	I			IV	V (V7)			

Here is what the I, IV, V, and V7 chords of C major look like:

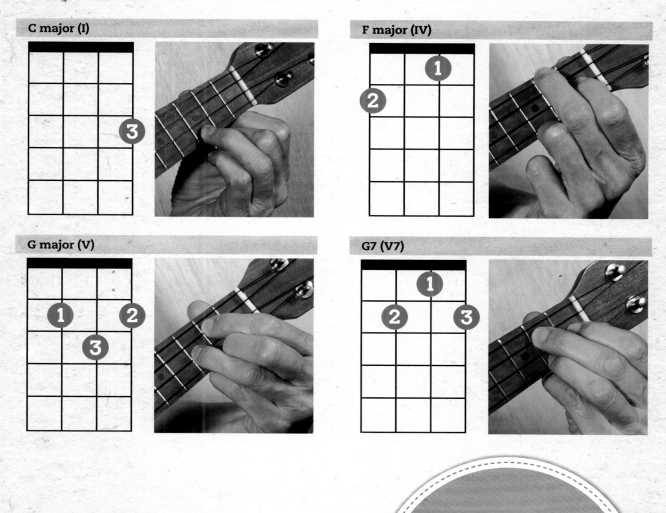

C major (I)

F major (IV)

G major (V)

G7 (V7)

Ukulele Tip:

An acoustic ukulele can be amplified using a condenser microphone or by adding a pickup to the instrument.

For the key of G, the chord pattern is G, C, and D or D7
(G is the first note of the scale, C the fourth, and D the fifth).

Notes in the scale	G	A	B	C	D (D7)	E	F	G
Chord number	I			IV	V (V7)			

Here is what the I, IV, V, and V7 chords of G major look like:

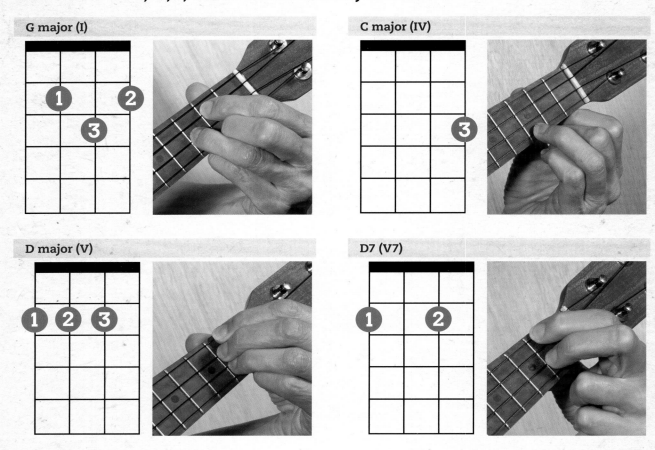

G major (I)

C major (IV)

D major (V)

D7 (V7)

Israel Kamakawiwo'ole

Israel Kamakawiwo'ole greatly influenced Hawaiian music through his ukulele playing. His fame spread outside Hawaii when his album "Facing Future," released in 1993, became the state's first certified platinum album, selling more than one million copies. Kamakawiwo'ole toured extensively in the United States and released fifteen successful albums during his lifetime. He is best known for his medley combining "Over the Rainbow" with Louis Armstrong's classic "What a Wonderful World," which has been featured in several films, television programs, and commercials. The Hawaii Academy of Recording Arts recognized his talent in 1997 with the awards Male Vocalist of the Year, Favorite Entertainer of the Year, Album of the Year, and Island Contemporary Album of the Year. Kamakawiwo'ole passed away in June 1997.

Here are some other common chord families:

A major chord family:

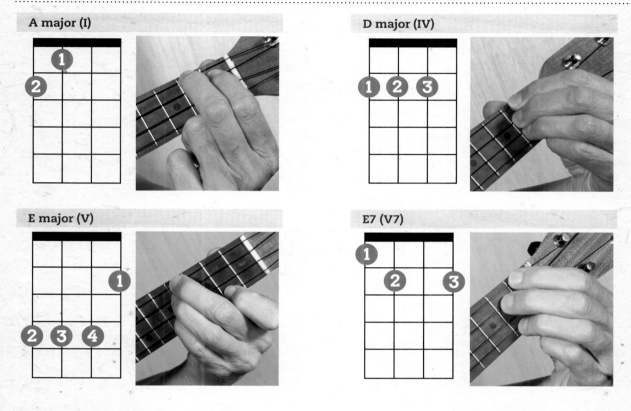

A major (I)

D major (IV)

E major (V)

E7 (V7)

F major chord family:

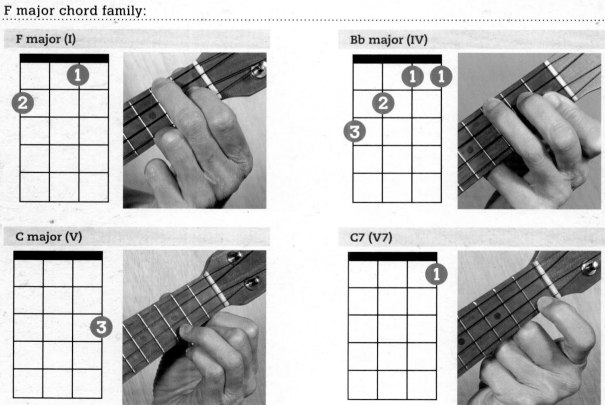

F major (I)

Bb major (IV)

C major (V)

C7 (V7)

There is often more than one way to play a chord. Here are two examples for alternative finger positions to play a C major chord. You can see other examples on the chord charts on pages 55–57.

C major on 3rd fret

C major on 7th fret

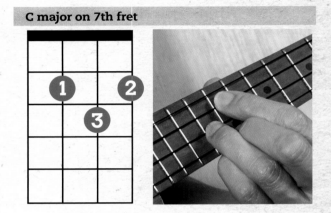

PLAYING BY EAR

Listen and Play Along
TRACK 7: PLAYING BY EAR

An experienced player can usually pick up the chord changes in a song just by listening. You will be able to do this, too, as practice trains your ear. In the meantime, it will help your playing if you listen to Track 7 and get the feel of certain types of chords.

You will hear a progression of C, F, and G chords, which happen to be the I, IV, and V chords in the key of C. The C chord most definitely has the comfortable feel of the "home" chord. The F chord has variously been described as the "stepping out" or "sunshine" chord. It

doesn't matter how you describe this IV chord, as long as you can grasp the different feel and sound that it has from the I chord. To my ear, the G, or V, chord has an "anxious" tone when played in this progression and begs to return "home" to the C chord. If it is played as a V7 chord (G7), then it sounds even more anxious.

Give your ear some training by listening to "Crawdad" (page 52, Track 17) and reading the chord changes as you listen to the song.

BAR CHORDS

A bar chord is just another way to play the same chord, but with a different sound to give you some variation to work with. Look at the examples below and observe the basic chord shapes under the bar. The G bar chord is actually the F chord moved down two frets with the forefinger acting as a nut. If you move the G bar chord down two frets, then it becomes an A chord, and so on.

Ukulele Tip:

If your strings begin to look worn, with nicks or grooves, it's time to replace them.

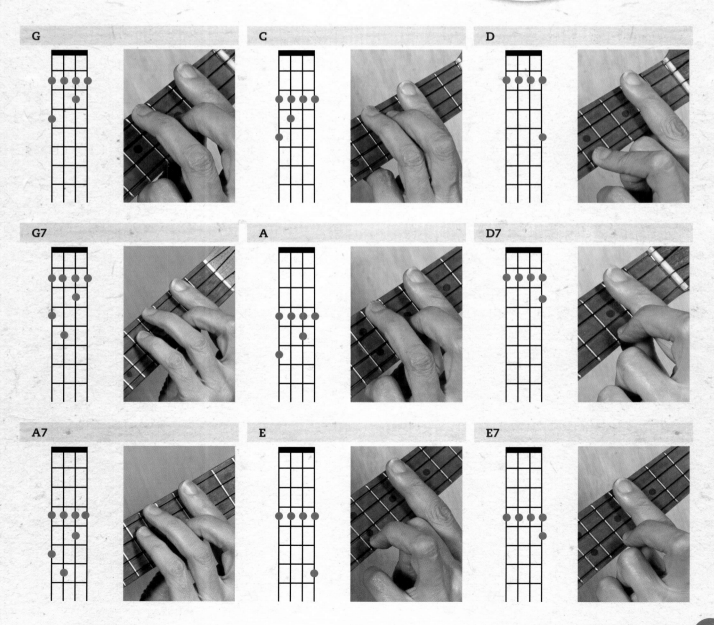

CHAPTER 6

12-Bar Blues

The 12-bar blues is a standard progression that forms the basis for a multitude of rhythm and blues and rock and roll songs. There are many variations on this basic progression, but the idea remains the same.

In the table below, each box represents one bar of 4/4 time, where the chord number is played on each beat.

The last bar (chord V or V7) is called the turnaround. It takes the song back to the next 12-bar sequence and so on, until everyone gets sick of playing, and then a I chord is used to finish the song. Of course, there are many variations of this common basic pattern.

Listen to some of your favorite songs and see how many you can find that exactly fit or are derived from the 12-bar blues pattern. Here are some examples:

- Blue Suede Shoes
- Hound Dog
- In the Mood
- Jailhouse Rock
- Johnny B. Goode
- Kansas City Blues
- Shake, Rattle, and Roll
- Sweet Home Chicago
- Tutti Frutti

A 12-bar blues session provides a great opportunity to improvise with bar chords, second and third position chords, and finger picking.

If we use the chord numbering system, the 12-bar progression looks like this:

First four bars	I/I/I/I	I/I/I/I	I/I/I/I	I7/I7/I7/I7
Second four bars	IV/IV/IV/IV	IV/IV/IV/IV	I/I/I/I	I/I/I/I
Final four bars	V/V/V/V	IV/IV/IV/IV	I/I/I/I	V/V/V/V

So, in the key of G, the progression is played like this:

First four bars	G/G/G/G	G/G/G/G	G/G/G/G	G7/G7/G7/G7
Second four bars	C/C/C/C	C/C/C/C	G/G/G/G	G/G/G/G
Final four bars	D/D/D/D	C/C/C/C	G/G/G/G	D/D/D/D

Listen and Play Along
TRACK 8: LEARN TO PLAY THE UKULELE OVERNIGHT BLUES

Playing the blues is really easy and a lot of fun. Using the chord progression on page 40, follow the recording and play the progression all the way through over and over. As the track progresses, you will hear that we add some words and a few mates will join in with other instruments. You can sing along to this song, which we call "Learn to Play the Ukulele Overnight Blues." Musically it may sound a bit complicated, but the basic progression will remain the same throughout. Keep playing. If you get lost, wait until the next round and start again. You may soon be able to recognize when each line of the progression starts on the CD.

When you listen on the computer, select an easy section and play it for a while in a repeating loop. You will find this feature available on the free download "VLC media player."

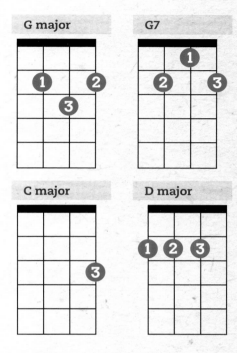

Chords:

For the first two lines of each verse, play G/G/G/G7. For the third line, play C/C/G/G. For the last line, play D/C/G/D.

Lyrics:

If you're sick of the TV, you got nothin' to do,
  Well listen up, baby, we've got something for you,
You can learn the ukulele, you can learn it overnight,
  So open up the book and we'll show you how to do it right,
First you tune up your uke and then you learn how to strum,
  You drive the cat crazy with that Brother John,
And your fingers are hurtin', and your arm is gettin' numb,
  The book has the nerve to tell you that this is all fun!
It's OK for the authors, 'cause they know all the chords,
  But we gotta practice 'til we're totally bored,
Then there's a scale pentatonic, whatever that may be,
  There's even 4/4 time and something called the key of C.
But the songs ain't half bad if you can just strum along,
  There's the midnight special and a sloop called John,
I know I'll learn to play, it won't take me long.
  I'll learn to lose these, learn to play the ukulele... overnight blues.

Ukulele Tip:
Low humidity can shrink wood and split your ukulele. Put a humidifier in your case.

CHAPTER 7

Songs

Here are some songs that you can use to practice all of the skills you've learned so far. You can mute your strings and strum along to the rhythm, listen to the song and try to pick out the chord changes, or play and sing along!

Ukulele Fact:

Jesse Kalima won the Hawaii Amateur Ukulele Championship in 1935 with his ukulele rendition of "Stars and Stripes Forever."

PHOTO BY IAN FISK.

Jamming. The best part about learning the ukulele is getting to play with others. Attending local jam sessions and ukulele festivals is a great way to learn.

Listen and Play Along
TRACK 9: POLLY WOLLY DOODLE

For this song, the first verse and chorus are played with a basic down strum in 4/4 time. Strum with the beat and emphasize the first beat of each bar. After that, try a mixture of down and up strums and be more adventurous with your strumming style. Sometimes the chorus incorporates a down up/down strum each time you sing the words "fare thee well." When this happens, play two down strums to complete the bar. For the most part, chord changes occur on the words "day" and "fey." Close the book and play by ear to see if you can pick the chord changes.

C major	F major

TIME SIGNATURE: TRADITIONAL 4/4 TIME

Intro

C/C/C/C, F/Rest/Rest/Rest. (That is, play C for four strums, then F for one strum, and rest for the remaining three beats. Then, begin the first verse.)

First verse

Oh, **F** *I went down south for to see my Sal,*

    Singing Polly Wolly Doodle all the **C** *day,*

My Sal, she is a saucy gal,

    Singing Polly Wolly Doodle all the **F** *day!*

Chorus

F *Fare thee well, fare thee well, fare thee well my fairy* **C** *fey,*

    Goin' to Louisiana,

For to see my Susyanna,

    Singing Polly Wolly Doodle all the **F** *day!*

Second verse

F *Behind the barn, down on my knees,*

    Singing Polly Wolly Doodle all the **C** *day,*

I thought I heard a chicken sneeze,

    Singing Polly Wolly Doodle all the **F** *day!*

Repeat Chorus

Third verse

F *Oh, a grasshopper sittin' on a railroad track,*

    Singing Polly Wolly Doodle all the **C** *day,*

Pickin' his teeth with a carpet tack,

    Singing Polly Wolly Doodle all the **F** *day!*

Repeat Chorus

Fourth verse

F *Came to a river and I couldn't get across,*

    Singing Polly Wolly Doodle all the **C** *day,*

I jumped on a gator 'cause I thought it was my hoss,

    Singing Polly Wolly Doodle all the **F** *day!*

Repeat Chorus

Song Book

Listen and Play Along
TRACK 10: PAY ME MY MONEY DOWN

Random picking with thumb and fingers suits the upbeat tempo of this song. There is a strong emphasis on striking the G string with the thumb, followed by a random pluck on any other string or strings on the upstroke. There is also an occasional light down strum on all the strings. At the finish, play an abrupt F chord. Try using a choke.

C7

F major

TIME SIGNATURE: TRADITIONAL 4/4 TIME

Intro

C7/C7/C7/C7, F/Rest/Rest/Rest

First verse

F *Thought I heard the captain say,*

   Pay me my **C7** *money down,*

Tomorrow is our sailing day,

   Pay me my **F** *money down.*

Chorus

F *Pay me, pay me,*

   Pay me my **C7** *money down,*

Pay me or go to jail,

   Pay me my **F** *money down.*

Second verse

F *The very next day he cleared the bar,*

   Pay me my **C7** *money down,*

He knocked me down with the end of a spar,

   Pay me my **F** *money down.*

Repeat Chorus

Third verse

F *Well, I wish I was Mr. Steven's son,*

   Pay me my **C7** *money down,*

Sit on the bank and watch the work done,

   Pay me my **F** *money down.*

Repeat Chorus

Fourth verse

F *Wish I was a rich man's son,*

   Pay me my **C7** *money down,*

Sit on the bank and watch the river run,

   Pay me my **F** *money down.*

Final chorus

F *Pay me, pay me,*

   Pay me my **C7** *money down,*

Pay me or go to jail,

   Pay me my **F** *money down.*

Instrumental Chorus

F *Pay me, pay me,*

   Pay me my **C7** *money down,*

Pay me or go to jail,

   Pay me my **F** *money down.*

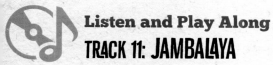
Listen and Play Along

TRACK 11: JAMBALAYA

Words and music by Hank Williams.

To give this song that country feel, try plucking the G string at the start of each bar, followed by a down strum for the second beat; repeat the pluck and strum to complete the bar. For your first try, you might like to substitute a G7 chord for G.

G major	G7	C major

TIME SIGNATURE: TRADITIONAL 4/4 TIME

Intro

G/G/G/G, G7/G7/G7/G7, C/C/C/C

First verse

C Good-bye, Joe, me gotta go, me oh **G** my oh,

    Me gotta go pole the **G7** pirogue down the **C** bayou,

My Yvonne, the sweetest one, me oh **G** my oh,

    Son of a gun, we'll have big **G7** fun on the **C** bayou.

Chorus

C Jambalaya, crawfish pie, filé **G** gumbo,

    'Cause tonight I'm gonna **G7** see my ma cher **C** amio,

Pick guitar, fill fruit jar, and be **G** gay-o,

    Son of a gun, we'll have big **G7** fun on the **C** bayou.

Second verse

C Thibodaux, Fontaineaux, the place is **G** a-buzzin,'

    Kinfolk come to see **G7** Yvonne by the **C** dozen,

Dress in style and go hog wild, me oh **G** my oh,

    Son of a gun, we'll have big **G7** fun on the **C** bayou.

Repeat Chorus

Third verse

C Settle down far from town; get me a **G** pirogue,

    And I'll catch all the **G7** fish in the **C** bayou,

Swap my mon to buy Yvonne what she **G** need-o,

    Son of a gun, we'll have big **G7** fun on the **C** bayou.

Final chorus

C Jambalaya, crawfish pie, filé **G** gumbo,

    'Cause tonight I'm gonna **G7** see my ma cher **C** amio.

Pick guitar, fill fruit jar, and be **G** gay-o,

    Son of a gun, we'll have big **G7** fun on the **C** bayou,

Son of a **G** gun, we'll have big **G7** fun on the **C** bayou.

Song Book

Listen and Play Along

TRACK 12: THIS TRAIN IS BOUND FOR GLORY

Of course this number has the "chunka" feel of a train. When you play in a group, you can mute the strings now and again to emphasize the train-like rhythm.

C major	G7	C7	F major

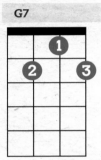
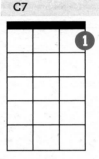
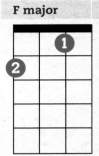

TIME SIGNATURE: TRADITIONAL 4/4 TIME

Intro

C/C/C/C, G7/G7/G7/G7, C/C/C/C

Chorus

C *This train is bound for glory, this train,*

This train is bound for glory, **G7** *this train,*

C *This train is* **C7** *bound for glory,*

F *Don't ride nothin' but the righteous and the holy,*

C *This train is* **G7** *bound for glory, this* **C** *train.*

First verse

C *This train don't carry no gamblers, this train,*

This train don't carry no gamblers, **G7** *this train,*

C *This train don't* **C7** *carry no gamblers,*

F *No hypocrites, no midnight ramblers,*

C *This train is* **G7** *bound for glory, this* **C** *train.*

Repeat Chorus

Second verse

C *This train is built for speed now, this train,*

This train is built for speed now, **G7** *this train,*

C *This train is* **C7** *built for speed now,*

F *Fastest train that you ever did see now,*

C *This train is* **G7** *bound for glory,* **C** *this train.*

Instrumental Chorus

Third verse

C *This train don't carry no rustlers, this train,*

C *This train don't carry no rustlers,* **G7** *this train,*

C *This train don't* **C7** *carry no rustlers,*

F *No street walkers, two-bit hustlers,*

C *This train is* **G7** *bound for glory, this* **C** *train.*

Repeat Chorus

Listen and Play Along
TRACK 13: MIDNIGHT SPECIAL

by Huddie Ledbetter

Experiment with this version of the D7 chord, sometimes referred to as the Hawaiian D7. This slow bluesy version will give you an opportunity to improvise around the basic 4/4 timing. Practice for your next jam by playing sparingly. Vary your strums and capture the feel of the song. Try some fast down/up strums mixed with down and up strums, and even miss playing the strings altogether.

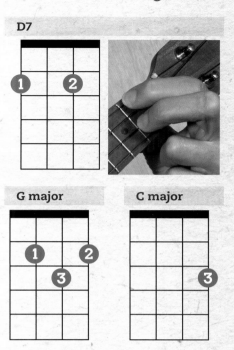

TIME SIGNATURE: TRADITIONAL 4/4 TIME

Intro

D7/D7/D7/D7, G

First verse

NO CHORD *When you wake up in the* **C** *morning,*

   Hear the ding-dong **G** *ring,*

You go marching to the **D7** *table,*

   You see the same old **G** *thing,*

Knife and fork are on the **C** *table,*

   Ain't nothin' in my **G** *pan,*

If you say a thing **D7** *about it,*

   You're in trouble with the **G** *man.*

Chorus

Let the midnight **C** *special*

   Shine a light on **G** *me,*

Let the midnight **D7** *special*

   Shine its ever-loving light on **G** *me.*

Second verse

NO CHORD *If you ever go to* **C** *Houston,*

   Boy you'd better walk **G** *right,*

You better not **D7** *gamble,*

   And you better not **G** *fight,*

Sheriff Benson will **C** *arrest you,*

   And he'll carry you **G** *down,*

And if the jury find you **D7** *guilty,*

   You're penitentiary **G** *bound.*

Repeat Chorus

Third verse

NO CHORD *Yonder comes Miss* **C** *Rosie,*

   How the world do you **G** *know?*

I can tell her by her **D7** *apron*

   And the dress that she **G** *wore,*

Umbrella on her **C** *shoulder,*

   Piece of paper in her **G** *hand,*

With a message for the **D7** *captain,*

   Turn loose my **G** *man.*

Repeat Chorus

Song Book

Listen and Play Along
TRACK 14: SLOOP JOHN B

Do nearly all the strumming with a relaxed forefinger and very little arm movement. A little practice will give you the sharp staccato sound that emphasizes the first beat of each bar and drives this song along. Once you have mastered the "groove," you can vary the strumming within the original arm movement. The strumming used in this song is more up strums than down. Listen for and copy the strum pattern: down, up/down/up, up/down. Try adding an occasional thumb pick on the G string.

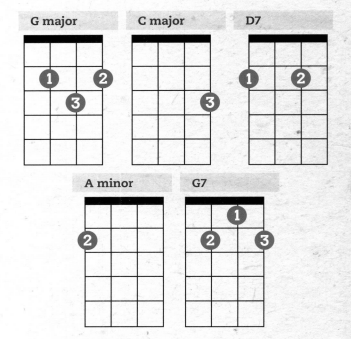

TIME SIGNATURE: TRADITIONAL 4/4 TIME

Intro

G/G/G/G, D7/D7/D7/D7, G/G/G/G

First verse

We **G** came on the sloop **C** John **G** B,

  My **G** grandfather **C** and **G** me,

Around Nassau town we did **D7** roam,

  Drinking all **G** night, **G7** we got into a **C** fight, **Am**

Well, I **G** feel so broke up, **D7** I want to go **G** home.

Chorus

So **G** hoist up the John **C** B's **G** sails,

  See how the main- **C** sail **G** sets,

Call for the captain ashore and let me go **D7** home,

  Let me go **G** home **G7**,

I wanna go **C** home **Am**,

  Well, I **G** feel so broke up, **D7** I wanna go **G** home.

Second verse

The **G** first mate he **C** got **G** drunk,

  And broke in the cap- **C** tain's **G** trunk,

Constable had to come and take him a- **D7** way,

  Sheriff John **G** Stone **G7**,

Why don't you leave me a- **C** lone **Am**,

  Well, I **G** feel so broke up, **D7** I wanna go **G** home.

Repeat Chorus

Third verse

The **G** poor cook he got **C** the **G** fits,

  And threw away all **C** of my **G** grits,

And then he went and he ate up all of my **D7** corn,

  Let me go **G** home **G7**,

Why don't they let me go **C** home **Am**,

  This **G** is the worst trip **D7** I've ever been **G** on.

Repeat Chorus

Listen and Play Along
TRACK 15: UKULELE LADY

Think about moonlit beaches and swaying palms when you're playing this song.

C major	C7	G major	G7	F major	D7

TIME SIGNATURE: TRADITIONAL 4/4 TIME

Intro

The introduction for this song is a simple riff played on the A string. Strum twice on the third fret, twice on the second fret, twice on the open string, and then twice on the second fret. Repeat.

Verse

If **C** you like Ukulele Lady, Ukulele Lady like-a you.

If **G7** you like to linger where it's shady, Ukulele Lady linger **C** too.

And **G7** she sees another Ukulele Lady fooling 'round with **C** you **C7**,

Repeat Twice

F Maybe she'll sigh,

C Maybe she'll cry,

D7 Maybe she'll find somebody else **G7** by and by.

To **C** sing to when it's cool and shady,

Where the tricky wicky wacky woo,

If **G7** you like Ukulele Lady, Ukulele Lady like-a **C** you.

(Sing the last line twice the second time through.)

Ukulele Tip:

Keep your strings free of oil buildup by wiping them occasionally with rubbing alcohol.

Song Book

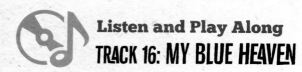

Listen and Play Along
TRACK 16: MY BLUE HEAVEN

Lyrics by George Whiting, music by Walter Donaldson, 1927.

This is a laid back song with lots of space in between the vocal lines, giving you the opportunity to experiment with your technique. If you are practicing a C scale, you can solo with the melody line or try some chord variations. You also have an opportunity to slide chords. For example, sliding the second position C chord means that you strike the chord shape on the second fret and, while it is ringing, slide up to the third fret.

Listen to the second position C chord immediately after the words "Mollie and me." After two strums of C, play the chord shape one fret closer to the nut, and then slide back to the C position. After the words "baby makes three," the second position C shape slides back toward the nut one fret for a strum and then back one more, followed by the A7 chord. This song is all about economy of playing.

Jamming with Strangers

The best part of playing the ukulele, or any instrument for that matter, is jamming with other people. It is scary at first, but something special always seems to happen once you overcome your fears. You will always play just that little bit better than before, and playing with others is a great way to train your ear.

Jam Hogs

Jam hogs are monsters who take over a jam session by playing their own choice of songs loudly and rudely. The good musicians soon drift off and the jam is ruined. But you, the beginner, can save the day. When there is a gap between songs, play around with the C major chord. The jam hog will duly ignore it and play over top of you. Keep at it. The others will encourage you to play. When you get your chance, strike up "Frère Jacques." Because you have been practicing, you will be playing your own exquisite version. Play quietly and elegantly. The *real* musicians will join in, adding their own vocals, instrumentals, chords, and riffs. The song will be sensational and the jam hog will scuttle off into the shadows from whence it came.

Here are a few tips for jamming:

- Get to the jam session early; that way, it is much easier to fit in.
- Play along quietly until you gain confidence.
- Listen to what is going on and add your music sparingly.
- Don't dominate the song list with all *your* favorites.
- Ask what key in which the song is being played and work out the main chords I, IV, and V (see page 34–35).
- If you are having trouble finding the chords, watch other players' fingers and copy the chord shapes until you get them.
- When you encounter a song that is too difficult, try muting your strings and strum along lightly to add percussion.
- Relax and enjoy the feeling of making music with friends.

The photo below shows the B chord. If you strum, then slide up one fret toward the body, you will have second position C. Listen for this cool slide in the first line after the word "call" and see what you can do.

Note another slide after the word "nigh." This time, the C shape is strummed, moved back to the second fret and strummed, then to the first fret for a strum. The final strum in the sequence is the one finger chord A7. Give that a go.

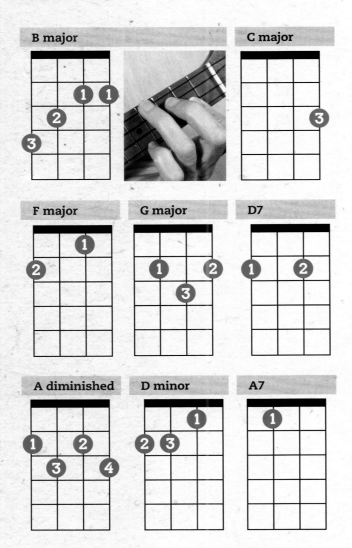

TIME SIGNATURE: TRADITIONAL 4/4 TIME

Intro

C major chord

Slides

Here are the slides you'll use in this song. Play each one a few times until you get the hang of it, and then try playing along.

SLIDE #1: Start by playing the B major chord shape on the third fret (C major). You will hold this chord shape throughout the slide. Strum on the third fret for three beats, slide to the second fret, strum once, and then slide back to the third fret and strum once.

SLIDE #2: Play a B major chord shape on the third fret (C major) and hold this shape through the slide. Strum for three beats, slide to the second fret, strum once, slide to the first fret, and strum once. Finish the slide with an A7 chord.

Verse (repeat twice)

C When whippoorwills call **SLIDE #1**, and evening is nigh **SLIDE #2**,

  I hurry to **D7** my **G7** blue **C** heaven.

C A turn to the right **SLIDE #1**, a little white light **SLIDE #2**, will lead you to

  D7 My **G7** blue **C** heaven.

A DIM You'll see a **F** smiling face,

  A7 A fireplace, a **Dm** cozy room **Dm7, Dm6**,

G A little nest that's **G7** nestled where the **C** roses **A DIM** bloom **G7**.

  Just Mollie and **C** me **SLIDE #1**, and baby makes three **SLIDE #2**,

We're happy in **D7** my **G7** blue **C** heaven.

Repeat the last line the second time you sing the verse. Finish with a G chord shape on the 7th fret, which is a C chord.

Song Book

Listen and Play Along
TRACK 17: CRAWDAD

This song sounds good when accompanied by some easy plucking and light brushing of the strings. You can add emphasis to the start of each bar by slapping the G string with your thumb. You can also try plucking the outside strings together at the beginning of each bar that starts on a C chord. Try hammering on the G string as you play the F chord.

Turn the CD down low and listen to what you are playing. This is a good song to learn how to jam with other people.

C major

F major

G7

C7

TIME SIGNATURE: TRADITIONAL 2/4 TIME

Intro

C/C/C/C, G7/G7/G7/G7, C/C/C/C

First verse

C *You get a line and I'll get a pole, honey,*

You get a line and I'll get a pole **G7***, babe,*

C *You get a line and* **C7** *I'll get a pole*

And **F** *we'll go down to that crawdad hole,*

C *Honey* **G7***, sugar baby* **C***, mine* **F C***.*

Second verse

C *Get up old man, you slept too late, honey,*

Get up old man, you slept too late **G7***, babe,*

C *Get up old man, you* **C7** *slept too late,*

F *Last piece of crawdad's on your plate,*

C *Honey* **G7***, sugar baby* **C***, mine* **F C***.*

Third verse

C *Get up old woman, you slept too late, honey,*

Get up old woman, you slept too late **G7***, babe,*

C *Get up old woman, you* **C7** *slept too late,*

F *Crawdad man done passed our gate,*

C *Honey* **G7***, sugar baby* **C***, mine* **F C***.*

Fourth verse

C *Along came a man with a sack on his back, honey,*

Along came a man with a sack on his back **G7***, babe,*

C *Along came a man with a* **C7** *sack on his back,*

F *Packin' all the crawdads he can pack,*

C *Honey* **G7***, sugar baby* **C***, mine* **F C***.*

Fifth verse

C *You get a line and I'll get a pole, honey,*

You get a line and I'll get a pole **G7***, babe,*

C *You get a line and* **C7** *I'll get a pole,*

And **F** *we'll go down to the crawdad hole,*

C *Honey* **G7***, sugar baby* **C***, mine* **F C***.*

C *Honey* **G7***, sugar baby* **C***, mine* **F C***.*

"Outro"

(Follow the tablature, as explained on page 32)

```
AI  -- slide from 2 up to 3-3-0-------
EI  ----------------------3-0---
CI  ------------------------0-
GI  -----------------------------
```

Follow the slide with a tremolo in C7.

Listen and Play Along
TRACK 18: HEY, GOOD LOOKIN'

Words and music by Hank Williams, Sr.

This classic is driven along by a solid beat that can easily be crushed by strum mania. Keep the rhythm going and replace some full strums with single-string strums using your fingers and thumb. Now and again, try a hammer on.

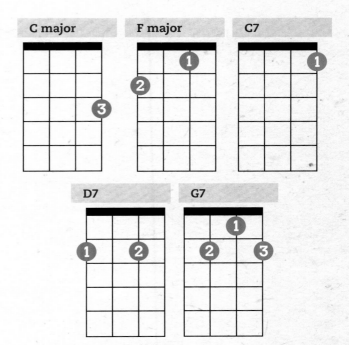

TIME SIGNATURE: TRADITIONAL 4/4 TIME

Intro

D7/D7/D7/D7, G7/G7/G7/G7, C/Rest/Rest/Rest

First verse

C Hey, good lookin', whatcha got cookin'?

   D7 How's about cookin' **G7** somethin' up with **C** me **G7**?

C Hey, sweet baby, don't you think maybe,

   D7 We could find us a **G7** brand new reci- **C** pe **C7**?

I got a **F** hot rod Ford and a **C** two dollar bill,

   F I know a spot right **C** over the hill,

F There's soda pop and the **C** dancin's free,

   So if you **D7** wanna have fun come a- **G7** long with me.

Chorus

C Hey, good lookin', whatcha got cookin'?

   D7 How's about cookin' **G7** somethin' up with **C** me?

Second verse

I'm **C** free and I'm ready so we can go steady,

   D7 How's about savin' **G7** all your time for **C** me?

C No more lookin,' I know I've been tooken,

   D7 How's about keepin' **G7** steady **C** company **C7**?

I'm gonna **F** throw my date book **C** over the fence,

   And **F** find me one for **C** five or ten cents.

F Keep it 'til it's **C** covered with age,

   'Cause I'm **D7** writin' your name down on **G7** ev'ry page.

Final Chorus

C Hey, good lookin,' whatcha got cookin'?

   D7 How's about cookin' **G7** somethin' up

D7 How's about cookin' **G7** somethin' up

   D7 How's about cookin' **G7** somethin' up with **C** me?

Song Book

Listen and Play Along
TRACK 19: AUSSIE BBQ

Words and music by Eric Bogle.
Copyright Larrikin Publishing. Used with permission.

This is a fast strum played under the vocals. Here's some Aussie vocab you might not recognize:

- Aeroguard = insect repellent
- Mossies = insects
- Esky = beer cooler
- Dunny = toilet

C major	F major	G major

TIME SIGNATURE: TRADITIONAL 4/4 TIME

Intro

G/G/G/G, C/C/C/C

First verse

C When the summer sun shines brightly on **F** Australia's happy land,

'Round **G** countless fires in strange attire you'll see many solemn **C** bands

Of glum Australians watching their **F** lunch go up in flames.

By the **G** smoke and the smell you can plainly tell, its barbie time **C** again.

Chorus

C When the steaks are burning fiercely, when the **F** smoke gets in your eyes,

When the **G** snags all taste of fried toothpaste,

And your mouth is full of **C** flies,

It's a national institution,

It's **F** Australian through and through,

So **G** come on mate, grab your plate,

Let's have a bar-b- **C** que!

Second verse

C The Scots eat lots of haggis, the **F** French eat snails and frogs,

The **G** Greeks go crackers over their moussaka, and the Chinese love hot- **C** dogs.

Welshmen love to have a leek, the **F** Irish love their stew,

But you **G** just can't beat, the half cooked meat of an Aussie bar-b- **C** que!

Third verse

C There's flies stuck to the margarine, the **F** bread has gone rock hard,

The **G** kids are fighting, the mossies are biting, who forgot the Aero- **C** guard?

There's bull ants in the Esky and the **F** beer is running out,

And **G** what you saw in mum's coleslaw you just don't think **C** about.

Repeat Chorus

Fourth Verse

C And when the barbie's over and your **F** homeward way you wend,

With a **G** queasy tummy on the family dunny, many lonely hours you **C** spend,

You might find yourself reflecting, as **F** many often do,

Come **G** rain or shine that's the bloody last time

You'll have a bar-b- **C** que!

Repeat Chorus

CHORDS

Here's a handy guide to all the chords used throughout this book.

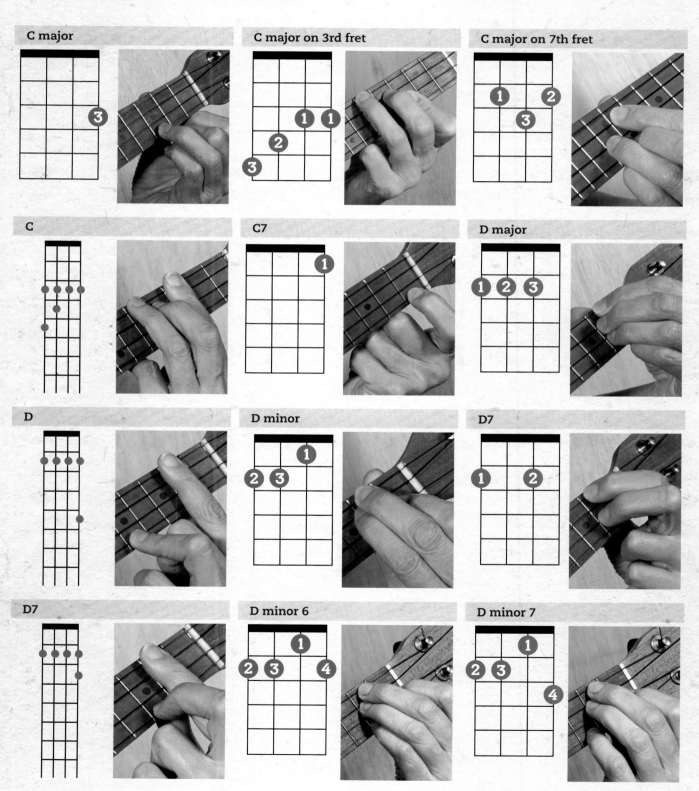

C major

C major on 3rd fret

C major on 7th fret

C

C7

D major

D

D minor

D7

D7

D minor 6

D minor 7

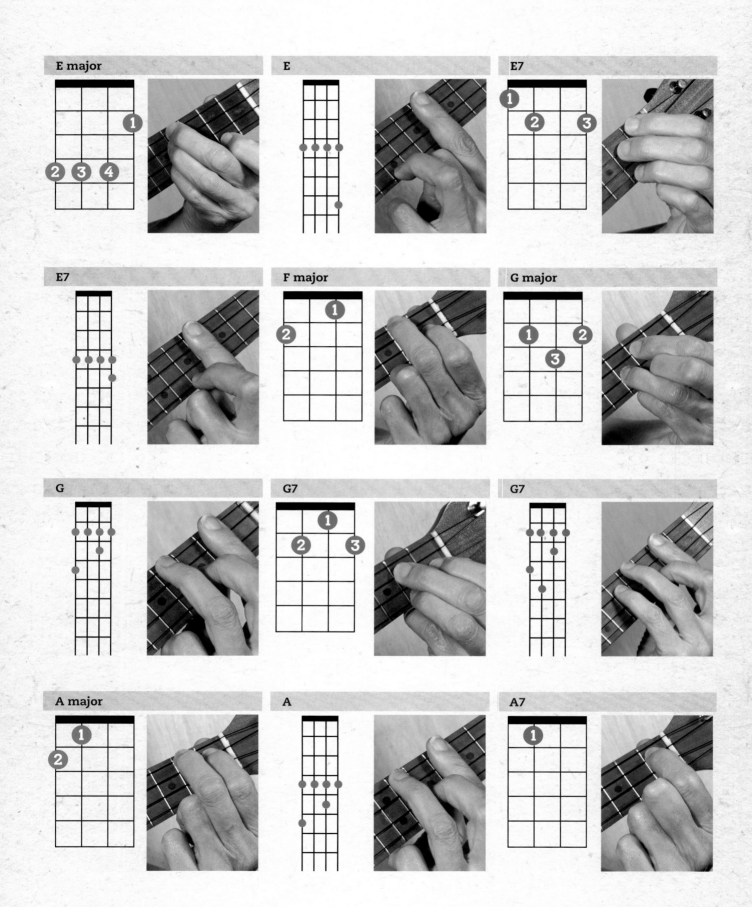

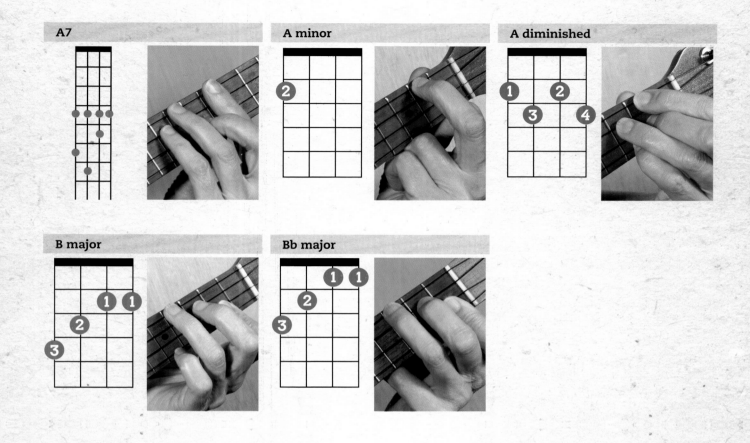

A7

A minor

A diminished

B major

Bb major

Tiptoe Through the Tulips

Born Herbert Khaury, Tiny Tim was a musician/singer who grew to popularity in the 1950s and 1960s. Khaury was known for performing popular songs with a strange twist, like his famous rendition of "Tiptoe Through the Tulips," which was accompanied by the ukulele. Khaury settled on his nickname in the early 1960s, and recorded an album titled *God Bless Tiny Tim* in 1968. He appeared on popular shows like *Laugh-In*, Johnny Carson's *Tonight Show*, the *Ed Sullivan Show*, the *Jackie Gleason Show*, and in the movie *You Are What You Eat*. He also appeared on *Conan* and the *Howard Stern Show*. Khaury died in November 1996.

PHOTO BY CHRISTINA LYNN JOHNSON

CHAPTER 8

The Ukulele Community

The ukulele is a wonderful way to bring people together, whether through jam sessions, community lessons or concerts, or large annual festivals. Do some research about the ukulele groups in your area, and check out the listing of ukulele festivals at the end of this chapter.

Ukulele Tip:

If you're traveling with your ukulele, don't leave it in an extremely hot or cold car.

PLAYING WITH A PURPOSE

We have found that there are many ways to reach out to others using the ukulele. Here are some of our experiences sharing the joy of music with others.

The carers

A dedicated group of selfless souls in our town has taken on the task caring for others, often family members, who are disabled or near death. These "carers" are on call around the clock and are often isolated, lacking proper support for themselves.

We are involved in a program that uses the ukulele as a medium to bring these people together so they can meet other carers, share their experiences, and express some of their feelings through music.

First, we teach them to sing and play a few of their favorite songs. Most of the carers are no strangers to the sing-along, and they only need to learn a couple of chords to participate. We then have them talk about all the funny, sad, frustrating, lonely, and joyous moments that come from being a carer. These moments are written into songs as a powerful means of expression.

The unassuming way the carers go about their tasks is remarkable. Their spirit, selfless dedication, strength of character, and stoic humor are humbling. It is great to see these people respond so positively to music.

One carer in the session is an octogenarian who looks after his wife. When his daughter picked him up one day, she said, "Dad was a new person last week when I took him home after the session."

Drought breaker

A few years ago we joined some other musicians for a weekend in a small town in the wheat belt, giving workshops to establish homemade music in the town. Everyone had a great time singing and learning to play various instruments, including the ukulele. We had some good sessions in the local bar and finished the weekend with a gala concert in the local concert hall.

Remarkably, the Department of Health funded the weekend because the small town had experienced many years of drought, which was affecting the health and wellbeing of its residents. The Department took the approach that good music is equal to good health.

Togetherness

The ukulele has been a wonderful way to bring people together in our town. As our first community ukulele project, we taught sixty people to play the instrument during an eight-week program. We organized three classes of twenty students, ranging in age from 7 to 82, with an equally wide range of abilities. The graduation concert held in the town hall was a sellout (free with afternoon tea provided).

About twenty to thirty students from the program organized a band that meets weekly to practice and socialize. The group plays at festivals, wine and food weekends, private functions, nursing homes, elderly citizens clubs, and, of course, at the local bar.

Sharing. Find some ukulele friends in your community and see how you can inspire others. Whether you're a group of three or a group of fifty, reach out and share the joy of music with those around you.

Helping others. We use the ukulele and music to help caregivers in our town. They learn to play, and to write songs that help express their feelings about the joys and frustrations of caring for others.

Accomplishments. The graduation concert held after our eight-week ukulele program was a huge success. Many of the program's graduates still meet to play together.

UKULELE FESTIVALS AROUND THE WORLD

Here is a listing of ukulele festivals worldwide, courtesy of the Ukulele Hunt website, *http://ukulelehunt.com*. Dates and times have a way of changing, and it has been known to rain. Check the details before you make reservations to attend a festival.

PHOTO BY DEB NEILL.

Ukulele fun. Ukulele festivals are held all over the world, bringing ukulele lovers together. Check for festivals in your area and don't miss the chance to attend. You'll connect with others, pick up some great tips and tricks, and get to jam all day long.

Ukulele Festival Hawaii

Ukulele Festival Hawaii, a non-profit organization, was started in 2004. Roy Sakuma, one of the organization's founders, orchestrated the First Annual Ukulele Festival in 1971. Roy and his wife, Kathy Sakuma, began UFH to share ukulele music with everyone, sponsoring festivals and music lessons throughout Hawaii. The organization also raises funds, which are returned as college scholarships and as free ukuleles for those who can't afford them. The organization sponsors four festivals every year on Oahu, Hawaii, Kauai, and Maui, which feature famous ukulele artists and other great musicians from around the world.

U.S. and Canada

Hayward, California
Ukulele Festival of Northern California
Performers, food, raffle, arts and crafts.
www.ukulelefestivalnorcal.org

St. Helena, California
Wine Country 'Ukulele Festival
Concerts, workshops, jam sessions,
open mic, concert/luau, wine tasting.
http://winecountryukefest.com

Tampa Bay, Florida
The Tampa Bay Ukulele Getaway
Performances, workshops, vendors,
raffle, jam sessions, luau.
www.tampabayukulele.com

Waikiki, Hawaii
Ukulele Festival Hawaii
Performers, vendors, food, ukulele
orchestra of eight hundred students.
www.ukulelefestivalhawaii.org

Waikoloa, Hawaii
Waikoloa Ukulele Festival
Performers, sing-alongs, ukulele
giveaways, food.
www.ukulelefestivalhawaii.org

Kahului, Hawaii
Maui Ukulele Festival
Performers, door prizes, food.
www.ukulelefestivalhawaii.org

Needmore, Indiana
Ukulele World Congress
Lessons, jam sessions,
performances, bonfire.
http://ukuleleworldcongress.wordpress.com

New Haven, Missouri
Mighty MO Riverfront Ukefest
Workshops, jam sessions, open mic,
vendors, performing artists.
www.mightymoukefest.com

Reno, Nevada
Play Uke Gatherings
Ongoing series of local concerts.
www.playuke.net

New York, New York
New York Uke Fest
Workshops, performers,
jam sessions, vendors.
www.nyukefest.com

Hood River, Oregon
Gorge Uke Fest
Concerts, jam sessions.
www.gorgeukuleles.org

Dallas, Texas
Lone Star Uke Fest
Open mic, workshops, concerts.
www.lonestarukefest.com

Vancouver, British Columbia
Ruby's Ukes
Ongoing series of workshops and events.
http://rubysukes.vpweb.ca

United Kingdom and Ireland

Cheltenham, England
Ukulele Festival of Great Britain
Performers, play-alongs, workshops,
vendors, food.
www.ukulelefestival.co.uk

Dublin, Ireland
Ukulele Hooley
Performers, workshops,
jam sessions.
www.ukulelehooley.com

Europe

Sint-Niklass, Belgium
Belgian Ukulele Festival
Concerts, jam sessions, open mic.
Visit the Belgian Ukulele Festival
page on Facebook.

Lerrain, France
*FIUL: Festival International
de Ukulele de Lerrain*
Jam sessions, open mic, workshops.
http://fiul.weebly.com

Paris, France
Ukulele Boudoir
Performers, workshops, classes.
http://festival.ukuleleboudoir.com

Bocholt, Germany
The Ukulele Hotspot Winterswijk
Concerts, open mic.

Barcelona, Spain
Ukefesta
Classes, concerts, open mic, jam sessions.
http://ukefesta.com/en

Australia and New Zealand

Cairns, Australia
Cairns Ukulele Festival
Performers, world's largest ensemble,
art exhibition.
http://cairnsukulelefestival.net

Melbourne, Australia
Melbourne Ukulele Festival
Performers, workshops, makers,
open mic, jam sessions.
www.muf.org.au

Katikati, New Zealand
Katikati Ukulele Festival
Performers, play-along, workshops,
open mic.

Asia

Thailand
Thailand Ukulele Festival
Performers, sing-a-long.
www.thailandukulelefestival.com

Websites and Creative Folks

SOME HANDY WEBSITES

If you want more information, songs, or a way to connect with other ukulele players, check out these sites:

Dr. Uke
This site has song sheets and MIDI tracks (standard electronic music, that is) that you can play along with.
www.doctoruke.com

The Fabulous Songbook
Here you'll find the words to just about every song you'll ever need to know.
http://kristinhall.org

Humble Uker Ramblings
This site is full of links to songs and other uke websites.
http://humbleuker.blogspot.com

Richard Gillmann's Free Ukulele Tab Links
Here you can find heaps of ukulele websites for songs, sheet music, and more.
http://nwfolk.com/uketabs.html

Steve's Beatles Page
The name says it all.
www.stevesbeatles.com

Taunton Ukulele Strummers
This site gives you a link to songbooks you can print for free.
www.tusc.co.uk

Ukulele Hunt
Here, you'll find a list of ukulele festivals and other great ukulele stuff.
http://ukulelehunt.com

Ukulele Boogaloo
This site includes links to organizations and clubs, performers' websites, instructional information, songbooks, and ukulele makers and retailers.
www.alligatorboogaloo.com/uke

Ukulele Underground: A Ukulele Forum
This site includes forums for beginners, contests, regional get-togethers, and more.
www.ukuleleunderground.com

UKULELE MAKERS

Check out the great work done by these ukulele makers by visiting them online.

Paul Celentano, North Carolina
www.etsy.com/shop/celentanowoodworks

Luke R. Davies, Australia
www.lukerdavies.com
lrdavies2@yahoo.com.au

Jerry Hoffmann, Missouri
www.boatpaddleukuleles.com

Peter Hurney, California
www.pohakuukulele.com

Jay Lichty, North Carolina
http://lichtyguitars.com

Daniel Luiggi, Argentina
www.luiggiluthier.com

Chuck Moore, Hawaii
www.moorebettahukes.com

Mya-Moe Ukuleles, Washington
www.myamoeukuleles.com

Keith Ogata, Hawaii
www.asdhawaii.com

Palm Tree Ukuleles, Colorado
http://palmtreeukuleles.com

Bill Plant, Australia
billplant23@gmail.com

Gary Zimnicki, Michigan
www.zimnicki.com

Index

ACQUISITION EDITOR: Peg Couch ● COPY EDITORS: Paul Hambke and Heather Stauffer ● COVER/LAYOUT DESIGNER: Jason Deller

DEVELOPMENTAL EDITOR: David Heim ● EDITOR: Katie Weeber ● PROOFREADER: Lynda Jo Runkle

More Great Books from Fox Chapel Publishing

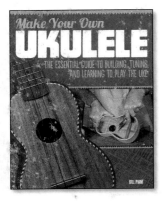

Make Your Own Ukulele
The Essential Guide to Building, Tuning, and Learning to Play the Uke
By Bill Plant

Learn how to make two different ukuleles, from a beginner's basic box-shaped uke, to a professional grade soprano ukulele.

ISBN: 978-1-56523-565-6
$17.95 • 96 Pages

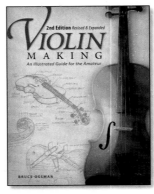

Violin Making, 2nd Edition
An Illustrated Guide for the Amateur
By Bruce Ossman

Make sweet music on a hand-crafted violin. All you need are just a few common tools, wood, and the simplified violin-making process found in this newly revised and updated book.

ISBN: 978-1-56523-435-2
$19.95 • 104 Pages

Handmade Music Factory
The Ultimate Guide to Making Foot-Stompin Good Instruments
By Mike Orr

Learn how to make eight of the most unique and imaginative instruments found anywhere - from a one-string guitar made from a soup can, to a hubcap banjo.

ISBN: 978-1-56523-559-5
$22.95 • 160 Pages

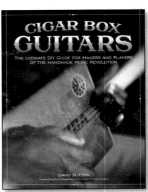

Cigar Box Guitars
The Ultimate DIY Guide for the Makers and Players of the Handmade Music Revolution
By David Sutton

Part DIY guide, part scrapbook—this book takes you behind the music to get a glimpse into the faces, places and workshops of the cigar box revolution.

ISBN: 978-1-56523-547-2
$26.95 • 200 Pages

The Wine and Beer Maker's Year
75 Recipes for Homemade Beer and Wine Using Seasonal Ingredients
By Roy Ekins

Join the thousands of amateur wine and beer makers in this enjoyable, cost saving hobby using seasonal ingredients and recipes to create great tasting beverages.

ISBN: 978-1-56523-675-2
$12.95 • 144 Pages

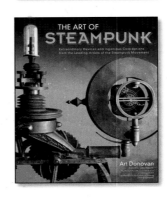

The Art of Steampunk
Extraordinary Devices and Ingenious Contraptions from the Leading Artists of the Steampunk Movement
By Art Donovan

Dive into the world of Steampunk where machines are functional pieces of art and the design is only as limited as the artist's imagination.

ISBN: 978-1-56523-573-1
$19.95 • 128 Pages

Labeling America: Popular Culture on Cigar Box Labels
The Story of George Schlegel Lithographers, 1849-1971
By John Grossman

Discover this historic collection of beautiful lithographic cigar box labels and bands from the 19th and 20th centuries, currently being housed at the Winterthur Museum in Delaware.

ISBN: 978-1-56523-545-8
$39.95 • 320 Pages

Natural Wooden Toys
75 Easy-To-Make and Kid-Safe Designs to Inspire Imaginations & Creative Play
By Erin Freuchtel-Dearing

Learn how to make safe, colorful, and irresistible imagination-building wooden toys. Step-by-step instructions show you how to make these charming designs, and how to create natural, non-toxic finishes.

ISBN: 978-1-56523-524-3
$19.95 • 184 Pages

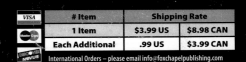